*serenity*

# *serenity*

## Ilene Kowis

Columbus, Ohio

*Serenity*

Published by Gatekeeper Press
2167 Stringtown Rd, Suite 109
Columbus, OH 43123-2989
www.GatekeeperPress.com

Copyright © 2022 by Ilene Kowis
All rights reserved. Neither this book, nor any parts within it may be sold or reproduced in any form or by any electronic or mechanical means, including information storage and retrieval systems, without permission in writing from the author. The only exception is by a reviewer, who may quote short excerpts in a review.

ISBN (paperback): 9781662929472

# Contents

Red Sands ............................................................... 6

Nothing .................................................................. 8

Aloha ................................................................... 10

The Mailman ...................................................... 12

Star on the Horizon ............................................ 14

Election Day ...................................................... 16

A Smile ............................................................... 18

Life of a Mother ................................................. 20

Silver Jubilee ...................................................... 22

Our Children ..................................................... 24

The Sunset ......................................................... 26

Time Passes ....................................................... 28

North Dakota .................................................... 30

My Husband ...................................................... 32

A Birthday Wish ................................................ 34

Just About Made It ............................................ 36

Seasons ............................................................... 38

What's Fair ........................................................ 40

My Father .......................................................... 42

Pretty Red Flowers ............................................ 44

One Six Pack and a Shot to Go ....................... 46

Alone .................................................................. 48

# Red Sands

It was first called Operation Desert Shield
With near 50,000 guys and gals in the field.
It's now called Operation Desert Storm
With everyone there true to form.
Army, Navy, Marines, and Air Force
Many others, we know of course.
They don't care to be in the sands
But brave and true they make their stand.
We at home can only hope and pray
That not too long will be their stay.
Please, Saddam, return to Iraq
So we can bring all our people back.
We need our fathers, sisters, and brothers,
Husbands, sons, and all the others.
Home is where they are needed
Don't let this plea go unheeded.
For years we've worked to do things right
To tear it down in one short night.
What will be gained in Desert Shield?
Why in this wonderful world no one can yield?
Does blood have to be shed, turning red the sand?
So much could be learned if we went hand in hand.

## Red Sands

It was at first called Operation Desert Shield
With near 500,000 guys and gals in the field.
Its now called Operation Desert Storm
With everyone there True to FoRM.
ARmy, Navy, Marines and Air Force
Many others, we know of course.
They don't care To be in the Sands
But brave and True they make their stand.
We at home can only hope and pray,
That not to Long will be their stay.
Please Saddam, Return To Iraq
So we can bring our people all back.
We need our fathers, sisters and brothers,
Husbands, sons and all the others
Home is where they are needed.
Don't Let this plea go unheeded.
For years we've worked to do things Right
To tear it down in one short night
What will be gained in Desert Shield?
Why in this wonderful world no one can yield?
Does blood have to be shed, Turning Red the Sand.
So much could be Learned, if we went hand in hand.

# Nothing

There are poems written 'bout war and peace,
There are poems written 'bout marriage and divorce.
There are poems written 'bout everything
Is there one written about nothing?

Have you ever felt like nothing?
Have you ever just done nothing?
Roaming 'round the world just doing nothing –
Getting tired of doing nothing.

Get up in the morning and do nothing
Walk around your home and do nothing
No one on tv is doing nothing
Stop and think, are you doing nothing?

Walking, talking, sleeping is something
Who can say they are doing nothing
Eating, sitting, standing is something
So you really are doing something.

Guess the poems already written
Are a lot better than this one.
But I just felt like doing something
So I wrote this poem about nothing.

## Nothing

There are poems written 'bout war and peace.
There are poems written 'bout marriage and divorce.
There are poems written 'bout everything
Is there one written about nothing?

Have you ever felt like nothing?
Have you ever just did nothing?
Roaming 'round the world just doing nothing —
Getting tired of doing nothing.

Get up in the morning and do nothing
Walk around your home and do nothing
No one on T.V. is doing Nothing
Stop and think, are you doing nothing?

Walking, Talking, Sleeping is something
Who can say they aren't doing nothing
Eating, sitting, standing is something
So you are really doing something.

Guess the poems already written
Are a lot better than this one.
But I just felt like doing something
So I wrote this poem about nothing.

# Aloha

The deep blue of Hawaiian skies
Birds that love to fly and fly.
Trees that grow so straight and tall
Rain that's soft when it falls.
Beautiful, warm, sandy beaches
Within everyone's life it reaches
Who loves the sun, it's all there
Lots of fun, no place can compare
An island made from God's great love
He left a sign, oh so great
An island of love He did create.

Pearl Harbor took a terrible toll
It touched the hearts and the souls
Of many people far and wide
North, South, every side
But beauty comes from love of all
No matter how big or small
Hawaii is the best of all
Really a land to have a ball.

## Aloha

The deep blue of Hawaiian skies
Birds that love to fly and fly.
Trees that grow so straight and tall
Rain thats soft when it falls.
Beautiful, warm, sandy beaches
Within everyones life it reaches.
Who loves the sun, its all there
Lots of fun, no place can compare
An island made from Gods great love
To share with us from above
He left a sign, oh so great
An island of love he did create.

Pearl Harbor took a terrible toll
It touched the hearts and the souls
Of many people far and wide.
North, South, every side
But beauty comes from love of all
No matter how big or small
Hawaii is the best of all
Really a land to have a ball.

# The Mailman

Over the hill and thru the dale
Every day to get the mail.
We all expect it to be there
Whether it rains, snows, or hails.

How in the world can a mailman stand it?
Whoever in the world gives him credit?
He's expected to be there on time every day
Always a smile, so happy and gay.

Never takes a coffee break
Never a rest from cold weather he takes.
Day after day, you'll see him go by
How does he do it, oh goodness, oh my.

We take everything for granted
If it's done wrong we rave and rant.
But when we do wrong
We fight back so strong.

So remember the mailman
Let's give him a hand.
When you see him go by
'Member he's a wonderful guy.

## The Mailman

Over the hill and thru the dale
Everyday to get the Mail.
We all expect it to be there
Whether it Rains, snows or hails.

How in the world can a mailman stand it?
Whoever in the world gives him credit?
He's expected To be there on time every day
Always a smile, so happy and gay.

Never takes a coffee Break
Never a Rest from cold weather he takes.
Day after day, you'll see him go By
How does he do it, oh goodness, oh my.

We take everything for granted
If its done wrong we Rave and rant.
But when we do wrong
We fight back so strong.

So Remember the Mail Man
Lets give him a hand
When you see him go By
'Member he's a wonderful guy.

# Star on the Horizon

Robert Kennedy, a fine young man,
Who was loved throughout the land.
He made it clear for all to hear,
What he would do if elected this year.

He travelled near, he travelled far,
Always bright like a shining star
Never too tired to shake a hand,
Never too tired to take a stand.

He knew the things that must be done
In the USA and Vietnam.
He had a chance to clear our land
To turn our troubles into something grand.

One man took Bob's wonderful life,
Leaving his children and saddened wife.
His mother and father who were so proud
To hear their son speak so loud.

Another great name to add to the list
For all to be remembered and all to be missed.
This world must not live in sorrow and pain
Or what they have died for will all be in vain.

Star on the Horizon                    6-6-68

Robert Kennedy, a fine young man,
Who was loved throughout the land.
He made it clear for all to hear,
What he would do if elected this year.

He traveled near, he traveled far,
Always Bright Like a Shining star
Never to Tired To shake a hand
Never To Tired To Take a stand.

He knew the things That must be done
In the USA and Viet Nam.
He had a chance To clear our Land
To Turn our Troubles into something grand.

One man Took Bobs Wonderful Life,
Leaving his children and saddened wife.
His mother and father who were so proud
To hear their son speak out so Loud.

Another great name to add to the List
For all to be Remembered and all to be missed.
This world must not Live in sorrow and pain
Or what they have died for, will all be in vain.

# Election Day

Come one, come all, it's election day,
Cast your vote, only your way.
The Democrats are on their way
Maybe they are here to stay.
The Republicans think they can lick
The one and only Mr. Big
Lots of money, lots of talk
Can only make a longer walk.
Doing is the important thing
Your vote will make the parties sing
Both are really on our side
In them then we will confide.

# Election Day

Come one, come all, it's election day,
Cast your vote, only your way.
The Democrats are on their way
Maybe they are here to stay.
The Republicans think they can Lick
the one and only Mr. Big
Lots of money, Lots of Talk
Can only make a Longer walk.
Doing is the important thing
Your vote will Make the parties sing
Both are really on our side
In them then, we will confide.

# A Smile

A smile can bring a thousand times
As much happiness as a million dimes
Money can never buy
What one smile can give a guy.

A smile a daughter gives her mother
Certainly there is no other.
The smile a son gives his father
Nothing else will ever bother.

A smile from a friend in the morning
Makes the heart go a soaring
A smile from a husband to his wife,
Makes a heart fill with life.

## A Smile

A smile can bring a thousand times
As much happiness as a million dimes
Money can never buy
What one smile can give a guy.

A smile a daughter gives her mother
Certainly there is no other.
The smile a son gives his father,
Nothing else will ever bother.

A smile from a friend in the morning
Makes the heart go a soaring
A smile from a husband to his wife,
Makes a heart fill with life.

# Life of a Mother

Up in the morning before the sun,
Knowing all the work to be done.
What to do first is the question at hand
In the kitchen Mother stands.

Then comes a rumble and a roar
It has to be a hundred or more.
Footsteps down the hall can be heard
After that it is just a blur.

What should I wear?
Oh goodness, my hair!
"I can't find my pants,"
I heard one of them chant.

Then at the table you look around
All of a sudden you know you've found
A life full of joy
With your girls and your boys.

The noise that they make
The neighbors they wake.
There can't be another
The life of a mother.

## Life of a Mother

Up in the morning before the sun,
Knowing all the work to be done.
What to do first is the question at hand
In the kitchen mother stands.

Then comes a rumble and a roar,
It has to be a hundred or more.
Footsteps down the hall can be heard,
After that it is just a blur.

What should I wear?
Oh goodness my hair!
I can't find my pants,
I heard one of them chant,

Then at the table you look around
All of a sudden you know you've found,
A life full of joy
With your girls and your boys.

The noise that they make
The neighbors they wake.
There can't be another
The Life of a Mother.

# Silver Jubilee

In Oklahoma, a west, south central state,
Mom and Pop were waiting their big fate.
Pops was walking 'round and 'round
When from somewhere came a beautiful sound.

A son was born that special date
Priesthood was to be his fate.
He went to school like other boys
And had his own special joys.

Then one day he stood straight and tall
And knew at last he'd heard his call.
He knew he wanted to become a priest
So off to school to try at least.

Finally he finished the long, last mile
There stood Father with a happy smile.
The bishop said, "You are a priest, in great need
Go into the world, do your worthy deed."

For twenty-five years he's been doing his thing
Happiness in his voice still rings.
He says he doesn't know how to sing
But during mass his words just may sting.

We know he likes goose and pumpkin pie
Usually on Sundays you can see him fly.
Hunting and golfing sometimes he will go
Any more, there's no need to know.

Special blessings on this day
Guard you well every step of the way.
Today we send this silent plea
Father, for your Jubilee.

*Dedicated to Fr. Adolph Pribyl (1921-1972)

Father Pribyl  Silver Jubilee

In Oklahoma, a west, south central state,
Mom and Pop were waiting their big Fate.
Pop's was walking 'round and 'round
When from somewhere came a beautiful sound.

A son was born that special date
Priesthood was to be his fate
He went to school like other boys.
And had his own special joys.

Then one day he stood straight and tall,
And knew at last he'd heard his call.
He knew he wanted to become a priest.
So off to school to try at least.

Finally he finished the long, last mile
There stood Father with a happy smile.
The bishop said, "You are a priest, in great need"
Go into the world, do your worthy deed

For twenty-five years he's been doing his thing
Happiness in his voice still rings.
He says he doesn't know how to sing
But during Mass his words just may sting.

We know he likes goose and pumpkin pie
Usually on Sundays you can see him fly.
Hunting and golfing sometimes he will go
Anymore, there's no need to know.

Special blessings on this day
Guard you well every step of the way.
Today we send this silent plea
Father for your Jubilee.

# Our Children

Debbie is our oldest girl
In our midst she is a pearl.
Such a tiny thing when she was born
Early on a chilly morn.

Pam is a different kind
One like that you'll never find.
Today so quiet, tomorrow so loud
Never a parent ever so proud.

Della is our blond haired miss
Fills the heart with so much bliss.
In our family she is the speller
No one ever has to help her.

Dean is our first born boy
He was like a little toy.
Now he's old enough to play ball
On the field he stands so tall.

Allan is our little nut
Would do so good with Jeff and Mutt.
Can't sit still when music he hears
What will happen in the next few years.

Paulette is our quiet dear
Very often you'll see her tears.
Seldom do you ever hear
Any of her inside fears.

Wally is our ray of light
Makes our days gay and bright.
Smallest one of the bunch
Guess who is first for his lunch.

## Our Children

Debbie is our oldest girl
In our midst she is a pearl.
Such a tiny thing when she was born
Early on a chilly morn.

Pam is a different kind
One like that you'll never find
Today so quiet, Tomorrow so loud
Never a parent ever so proud.

Della is our blonde haired Miss
Fills the heart with so much bliss
In our family she is the speller
No one ever has to help her.

Dean is our first born boy
He was like a little toy
Now he's old enough to play ball
On the field he stands so tall.

Allan is our little nut
Would do so good with Jeff and Mutt.
Can't sit still when music he hears
What will happen in the next few years.

Paulette is our quiet dear
Very often you'll see her tears
Seldom do you ever hear
Any of her inside fears.

Wally is our Ray of Light
Makes our days gay and bright
Smallest one of the bunch
Guess whose first for his lunch.

# The Sunset

On the 20<sup>th</sup> of November
T'was an evening to remember
The sunset in the western skies
Was a sight for all man's eyes

It was blue, green, and coral pink
As the sun began to sink
Behind all the rolling hills
One's heart almost overfills.

Standing by the window
All the colors seem to flow
Through the window into the heart
Giving one an extra start.

If everyone could really see
What this sunset meant to me.
It cannot be explained by anyone
For now it's here and then it's gone.

## The Sunset

On the 20th of November
T'was an evening to Remember
The sunset in the Western skies
Was a sight for all man's eyes

It was blue, green and coral pink
As the sun began to sink
Behind all the rolling hills
Ones heart almost overfills.

Standing by the window
All the colors seem to flow
Through the window into the heart
Giving one an extra start.

If everyone could really see
What this sunset meant to me.
It cannot be explained by none
For now its here and then its gone

# Time Passes

What do you do when you're down in the dumps?
How do you get over life's terrible bumps?
We get depressed and ever so low
Especially in the winter when the cold winds blow.

The house gets so lonely
And wish we could only
Get out and play like the kids
Or go to a sale and make a bid.

Anything but the daily routine
Gee, that sounds ever so keen.
Days seem to pass us by
The months, the years seem to fly.

Where has the time gone?
Has it all been done wrong?
So many more things
The years seem to bring.

## Time Passes

What do you do when your down in the dumps
How do you get over Lifes terrible bumps
We get depressed and ever so low
Especially in the winter when the cold winds blow.

The house gets so Lonely
And wish if we could only
Get out and play Like the Kids
Or go to a sale and make a bid.

Anything but the daily routine
Gee, that sounds ever so keen.
Days seem to pass us by
The months, the years seem to fly.

Where has the time gone
Has it all been done wrong?
So many more things
The years seem to bring.

# North Dakota

There isn't much written about North Dakota
Some have never heard of the hop or the polka
The quiet towns and rodeo grounds
Give North Dakota its wonderful sounds.

The beautiful sunsets
The sounds of the jets
Up in the sky
They meet the eye.

In the morn the birds start to sing
All the clocks start to ring
Everyone is up to start the day
In order for the bills to pay.

No hustle and bustle for buses to catch
Big cities here could never match
North Dakota is quiet and serene
Sometimes white and sometimes green.

## North Dakota

There isn't much written about North Dakota
Some never heard of the hop or the polka
The quiet towns and rodeo grounds
Gives North Dakota its wonderful sounds

The beautiful sunsets
The sounds of the jets
Up in the sky
They meet the eye.

In the morn the birds start to sing.
All the clocks start to ring
Everyone is up to start the day.
In order for the bills to pay.

No hustle and bustle for buses to catch
Big cities here could never match.
North Dakota is quiet and serene
Sometimes white and sometimes green.

# My Husband

My husband is a wonderful man
Who's there with ever so tender hands
Early in the morning light
Off to work merry and bright.

From early morn 'til late at night
Works so hard with all his might
To see we get the things we need
All the children he will feed.

The days are so long and dreary
At night he's tired and weary
But sunshine follows him everywhere
A man like that is very rare.

He's always good and oh so kind
And never, ever seems to mind
Whatever is the unexpected
I'm never worried or unprotected.

## My Husband

My husband is a wonderful man
Whose there withever so tender hands
Early in the morning light
Off to work merry and bright.

From early morn 'til late at night
Works so hard with all his might
To see we get the things we need
All the children he will feed.

The days are so long and dreary
At night he's tired and dreary
But sunshine follows him every where.
A man like that is very rare.

He's always good and oh so kind
And never, ever seems to mind.
What ever is the unexpected
I'm never worried or unprotected.

# A Birthday Wish

Ever since the day I knew
You loved me and I loved you,
You've been in all my thoughts and dreams
In all my happy hopes and schemes.
And as I set your day apart
And celebrate it in my heart,
I'm thinking as I often do
How much life means because of you.

## A Birthday Wish

Ever since the day I knew
You loved me and I loved you
You've been in all my thoughts and dreams
In all my happy hopes and schemes
And as I set your day apart.
And celebrate it in my heart.
I'm thinking as I often do
How much life means because of you.

## Just About Made It

'Twas the night before graduation
And all through the school
Everything was set for summer vacation
The desks all scrubbed down
The rooms shone, oh so bright
You'd never guess there was nine months of fright.

The seniors crept in, to look at the gym
One more time they said with a cheer
We've done it, we've made it, now we're in the clear.

Tomorrow we come with our caps and our gowns
With best behavior we will be known
The screaming, the yelling, we heard all last year
We pass to the others, with dread, and with fear.

We're done, we've 12 years behind us
The diplomas will remind us
We've done it, we've made it
Thought never to see it.

All of a sudden, up in the office
The superintendent's laugh could be heard
We wondered why he was up there so late
Then what we heard put the fear in us all

"We'll see most of you back here come next year."

## Just About Made It

Twas the night before graduation
And All through the school
Everything was set for summer vacation
The desks All scrubbed down
The rooms shone, oh so bright
You'd never guess there was nine months of fright.

The seniors crept in, To Look at the gym
One more time they said with A cheer
We've done it, we've made it, now we're in the clear.

Tomorrow we come with our caps and our gowns
With best behavior we will be Known
The screaming, the yelling, we heard all Last year
We pass to the others, with dread, and with fear.

We're done, we've 12 years behind us
The diploma's will Remind us
We've done it, we've made it
thought never to see it.

All of a sudden, up in the office
The Superintendents Laugh could be heard
We wondered why he was up there so Late
Then what we heard put the fear in us all
"We'll see most of you, back here, come next YEAR.

# Seasons

Seasons seem to come and go
Rivers rise, run, and flow
Spring brings flowers, bright and gay
Trees so green, seem to glow
The children out to play
Summer sends out Mr. Sun
To the water everyone runs
Trying to cool the sunburned arms
Only to find it does more harm.
Fall is good, so they say
To rake the leaves you will pay
All cleaned up, the yard looks great
We know what will be our next fate
Winter comes, the wind starts to blow
The place fills up with pure white snow
The temperature falls, oh so low.
You wonder if you will ever see the rivers flow.

# Seasons

Seasons seem to come and go
Rivers Rise, Run and flow
Spring brings flowers bright and gay
Trees so green, seem to glow
The children out to play
Summer sends out Mr. Sun
To the water everyone runs
Trying to cool the sun burnt arms
Only to find it does more harm.
Fall is great so they say
To rake the leaves you will pay
All cleaned up the yard look's great
We know what will be our next fate
Winter comes, the wind starts to blow
The place fills up with pure white snow
The temperature falls, oh so low.
You wonder if you will ever see the rivers flow.

# What's Fair

Everyone loves their homeland
No matter where they stand
The flags that fly, remind us that we are free
We seem to forget what it took to get here,
The pain, the struggle of earlier years.
So much we've taken for granted
Those who want more we hear raving and ranting
Be thankful for all we have here today
Think of the ones who had to pay
The price for our lives we are living right now
Our heads each day should bow.
The arguing, the fighting all over the world
Yet no one gives in,
Lest someone else should win
Too many want wealth
While others pay with their health
The starving, the homeless, go on day after day,
Hoping to hear someone else say
"The price is too high,
When you hear our children cry, I'm hungry, I'm sad,
Come our country's turned bad."
Money won't buy the blue of the sky
Or the love we all share.
If only we'd stop and think what is fair.

## What's Fair

Every one loves their home land
No matter where they stand
The flags that fly, Remind us that we are free
We seem to forget what it took to get here.
The pain, the struggle of earlier years.
So much we've taken for granted
Those who want more we hear Raving and ranting
Be thankful for all we have here today
Think of the ones who had to pay
The price for our lives we are living right now
Our heads each day should bow.
The arguing, the fighting all over the world
Yet no one gives in,
Lest some one else should win
Too many want wealth
While others pay with their health
The starving, the homeless, go on day after day.
Hoping to hear someone else say
"The price is to high,
When you hear our children cry, I'm hungry, I'm sad, How
come our countries turned bad."
Money won't buy the blue of the sky
Or the love we all share.
If only we'd stop, and think what is fair.

# My Father

Such a kind and gentle man,
My father and my very best friend.
Things he said were just like a trend,
For man of the year he could certainly have ran.

Who could know when the telephone rang,
That quiet Thursday afternoon.
All the heartache and the fangs,
Of a death that came too soon.

He left me here to do the things,
He taught me all these many years.
The happiness a smile can bring,
That sadness only brings on tears.

No matter what I ever said,
He always was there to understand.
Knowing now that he is dead,
I only wish that I had said.

Told him how I really loved him,
With all my heart and soul.
Helped him with his every whim,
Helped him reach his topmost goal.

Now the flowers are brown and dry,
The ground so hard and cold.
All that is left is a silent cry,
To beg for help to make me bold.

I cannot look back,
Only straight ahead.
The heavy burden only I can pack,
Forever remembering my father's dead.

# My Father
### March 27, 1968

Such a kind and gentle man,
My father and my very best friend.
Things he said were just like a trend,
For man of the year he could certainly have ran.

Who could know when the telephone rang,
That quiet Thursday afternoon.
All the heartache and the pangs,
Of a death that came too soon.

He left me here to do the things,
He taught me all these many years.
The happiness a smile can bring,
That sadness only brings on tears.

No matter what I ever said,
He always was there to understand.
Knowing now that he is dead,
I only wish that I had *said*

Told him how I really loved him,
With all my heart and soul.
Helped him with his every whim,
Helped him reach his top most goal.

Now the flowers are brown and dry
The ground is hard and cold
All that is left is a silent cry
To beg for help to make me bold.

I cannot look back,
Only straight ahead.
The heavy burden only I can pack
Forever remembering my fathers dead.

## Pretty Red Flowers

P - retty red flower
O - ft time to remember
P - eople we don't even know
P - eople that now lay in a row
I - nside there is a soldier
E - ach with a story to tell
S - o when you see that little red flower, just remember.

Pretty Red Flowers

Of Time to Remember

People we dont even know

People that now Lay in a Row

inside there is a soldier

Each With a story to tell

So when you See A Little red Flower

Just Remember

# One Six Pack and a Shot to Go

Give me a six pack and a shot for the road
My goodness, I really feel bold.
I must be a king or a queen
Who was it that said, I'm always so mean?
How glad I feel, back of the wheel
Wonder how much rubber old Jessie would peel.
The lines on the highway looked like dots
Or a train with little white spots
A little red light came up from behind
Someone must have gone out of his mind.
They got me, how about that?
I hit the tree with a splat
Well, one dollar to blow on a six pack to go.
Was it worth it?
I guess no one will ever know.
I'll come back again someday for the show.
'Till then, you can have my six pack to go.

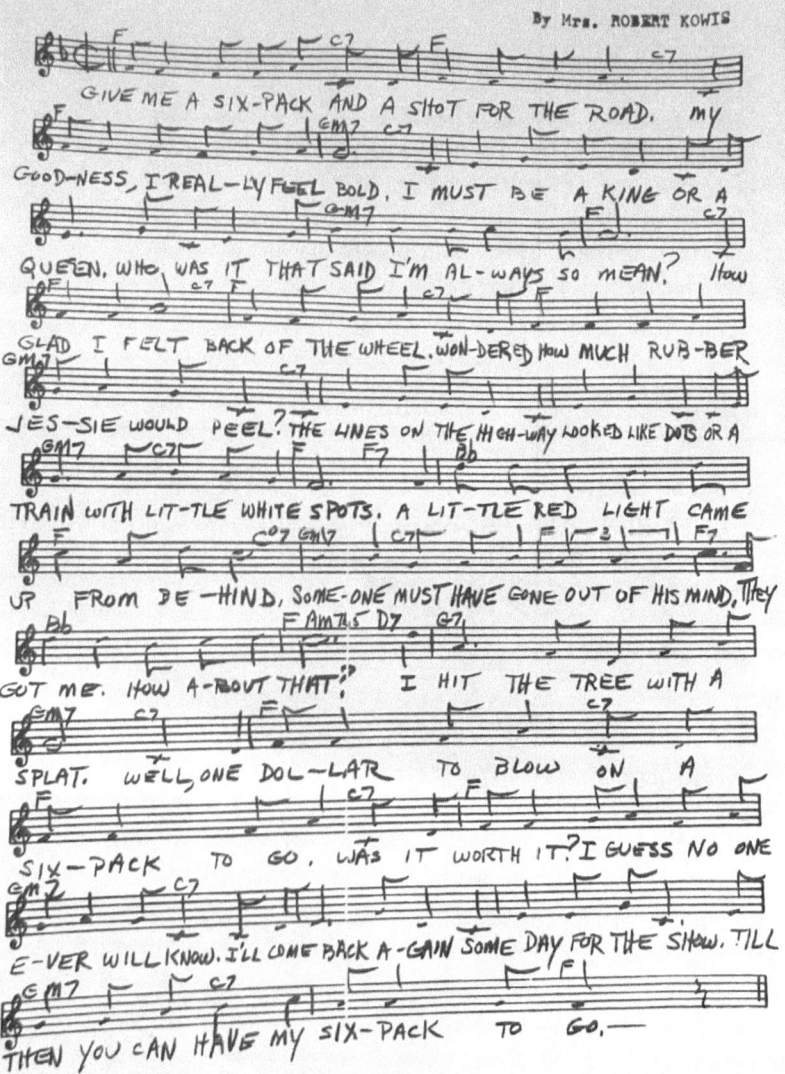

# Alone

Tonight I sit here all alone, my love
You never came home.
Days are so long, but I try to be strong
Have you gone forever? I hope I'm wrong.
How long must I sit here?
How long must I wait?
Will you come back, or have you found a new mate?
Was marriage just a game you found too tame?
How long must I wait for you to call my name?
Whether it's right or wrong, I know you're really gone.
Come back, my dear, and you'll see
My love for you will always be.
How long must I wait here alone and blue?
How long will you be forever true?
My arms are so empty since you left me.
Your true love forever I'll be.

www.ingramcontent.com/pod-product-compliance
Lightning Source LLC
LaVergne TN
LVHW042004060526
838200LV00041B/1863